What Our Readers Have Said...

"The Pinpoint Training Series delivers information that could be used in a lot different areas."

•

"Applicable and valid. The information is good."

•

"I like this because I can take them with me to read at a convenient time. I feel the little time I have to spend in the office is best use on activities that directly relate to revenue opportunities. I like the short amount of time it takes to keep up with these."

•

"I just read each book, and then file it for future reference."

•

"My thought is that the real value of these books comes into effect when doing the action plans."

•

"The challenge when I think a specific topic does not apply is to find a way to make it apply."

•

"Easy to use, understand, and reference if needed."

•

"Good layout and to the point."

•

"I think a lot of the recommendations in these books are very useful, and can be applicable to everyday situations. If nothing else, it's a good reference guide to fall back upon if a situation arises in the future."

•

"These books are relevant to today's work environment and the ongoing change in the way we manage our workforce."

•

"These books will pay for the time that I am investing. There are numerous good ideas that will streamline what I do and how I do it."

•

"All and all I think the Pinpoint series is a good program. I know other people I would love to have something like this. I think a lot of the suggestions are very useful, and can be applicable to everyday situations. If nothing else it's a good reference guide to fall back upon if a situation arises in the future."

•

"These books reinforce many concepts that I have learned through seminars, schooling and other programs. For myself, it serves as a constant learning tool that keeps me on top of the issues that many of us encounter every day."

•

"All in all, I think you have good training books. It helps everyone to review these materials, it serves as a good reminder to us on how to conduct ourselves."

•

"The information is valuable in these books."

•

"Good thoughts and ideas."

•

"I believe these books would be valuable to all employees."

•

Leadership

Pinpoint Management Skill Development Training Series

TIMOTHY F. BEDNARZ

MAJORIUM
BUSINESS PRESS

Pinpoint Management Skill Development Training Series
"Leadership"
Timothy F. Bednarz

Graphic design: Monika Pawlak

Majorium Business Press
2025 Main Street
Stevens Point, WI 54481
715.342.1018 • 800.654.4935

ISBN 978-1-882181-42-1

Printed in the United States of America

Introduction

The Pinpoint Management Skill Development Training Series is designed for targeted training and education regarding increased improvement in a specific skill or competency.

Each book within this series is designed to be easy to use, understand and apply to your job. It can be used as a basis for training individuals, as a discussion guide or as a personal training tool.

Each chapter within this book discusses a specific concept. When you have completed all eight chapters you should have a 360° perspective of the topic.

Additionally, each chapter is divided into specific sections:

- The first section provides you with an overview of the topic
- The Implications section discusses why the concept is important, and why it is important to learn and apply.
- The Strategies, Tips & Techniques to Apply section teaches how to use and apply the particular concept to your work.
- The Points to Ponder section gives you something to think about or to be discussed with a group setting. These are questions not meant to be immediately answered, but to be pondered over time.
- The Training Activity section provides you with the tools to transfer what you have learned to your job. It is designed to help create an action plan to effectively apply the concept.

Each of the topics in this series is time-tested and proven in the marketplace. They have been used by thousands of employees as training tools. Many of the users have commented that what made these books valuable, was the ability to refer to them when a problem surfaced. They indicated that they remembered reading about the exact problem. They referred back to these books and found an appropriate solution.

You will find them equally valuable as a resource in your professional development library.

Table of Contents

LEARNING OBJECTIVES:

- The principles of leadership.
- To identify their leadership potential.
- To develop an effective management style.
- To develop an effective leadership plan.

1

Learning to Be a Leader

There is a critical and substantial difference between managing to lead and managing to supervise. Managers who lead show others the way, while managers who supervise tend to direct and control. Leaders are individuals who motivate and inspire the individuals around them, whether they are coworkers or employees.

People often believe that "leaders are born not made," but this is far from the truth. Most people who have the desire and internal motivation can learn to incorporate effective leadership skills into their style of management. Doing this often includes making changes and alterations in mindsets and attitudes, without which many managers will never become the type of leaders others want to follow.

IMPLICATIONS — WHAT THIS MEANS TO YOU

Individuals who fall into the category of traditional supervising managers find themselves generally directing and controlling the people under them. They tend to be rigid in their thinking, ineffective and unproductive when compared to managers who are also leaders.

Managers as leaders are excellent motivators. They are more productive because they are able to tap into individuals as key organizational resources and rely on their cooperative efforts and results to get things accomplished effectively and efficiently. They ultimately assume cheerleader roles to inspire employees to greater heights of achievement. Most managers are surprised by how much more their departments and units are able to accomplish when they are effectively led.

If managers wish to achieve higher levels of results, they must learn to delegate various responsibilities to their employees and motivate them, rather than simply use control management methods. Due to higher expectation levels, results then tend to increase. Managers as leaders make certain that employees become empowered to accomplish more through greater levels of autonomy and responsibility. Most importantly, this change allows managers more time to concentrate on the important strategic issues affecting their entire department rather than focusing on daily tactical issues that can just as easily be delegated to individual employees.

STRATEGIES, TIPS & TECHNIQUES TO APPLY

Managers who lead are motivated by their own personal vision of what is possible to achieve. They are always focused on the accomplishment of major long-term goals. These goals provide them with deeply held convictions of what they desire to attain and how to go about achieving it. Their personal determination and perseverance are what attracts others to their vision and motivates them to not only believe in them, but also to embrace their attainment. Traditional managers, on the other hand, do not generally have these convictions or a vision for the future due to their having chosen to operate in a more reactive rather than proactive manner.

Managers as leaders inspire the active participation of individual employees by communicating their vision in a clear and convincing manner. Everything they say and do effuses passion and enthusiasm, which become contagious. Managers who lead are able to easily articulate their message and frequently "talk up" their personal vision. They work to create mental images of their vision that employees can conceptually see and feel.

Managers as leaders tend to have positive self-images. This affirmative sense of self translates into confidence and a keen awareness of their personal capabilities. These managers tend to build and develop similar characteristics in their employees by delegating and effectively sharing their power and professional knowledge. This is in direct contrast to more traditional managers who generally tend to hoard power and information, feeling that any form of delegation undermines their power base and authority.

Many managers are results-oriented with a zero-tolerance for mistakes and failure. This results in employees hiding their failures for fear of possibly severe repercussions. They tend to cover errors and misjudgments by altering information or misleading managers regarding certain results or oversights. This is one of the leading causes of managers being blindsided by unforeseen events and circumstances.

Leading managers, on the other hand, view mistakes and failures as learning experiences. They understand that they and their employees cannot grow and stretch their abilities without making mistakes and failing. They consistently encourage employees to implement new ideas, concepts and approaches and stretch their individual capabilities in order to learn from mistakes. This often produces more results-driven atmospheres than those seen through strictly supervisory management styles and practices. It enables leaders and their departments or units to react faster to evolving conditions and even anticipate certain changes before they produce negative impacts.

Managers who lead their people build trust and rapport through various mutual learning experiences, which are generally accompanied by trial-and-error approaches and outcomes. They are quick to listen and observe throughout the process, with one of their most positive attributes being their ability to offer appropriate feedback in non-threatening ways.

POINTS TO PONDER — SOMETHING TO THINK ABOUT

1. What is your personal style: traditional manager or effective leader?
2. Do you have any fears in regard to delegating some of your power, authority and knowledge? If so, what are they?

TRAINING ACTIVITY — APPLICATION & ACTION PLAN

1. Develop a vision for yourself by exploring the possibilities that you, your people and company can achieve. Think "outside of the box" in determining what you can accomplish in your particular department or unit.
2. When you have done this, write your vision down (a good vision statement should ideally fit on the back of a business card) and polish it until you are able to easily and effectively articulate it.

2

Identifying Your Leadership Potential

Despite the "leaders are born not made" axiom, with sufficient desire all individuals can generally become effective and productive leaders.

Everyone has leadership potential. Leaders make mistakes like anyone, but they have the humility and discipline to analyze why and how they were made, and learn from them so that they are not repeated.

The one characteristic leaders need to skillfully apply is their ability to continually stretch their own and their employees' capabilities and abilities. Managers as leaders learn to be innovative while relying on their employees and trusting in them to do the right thing. This is what distinguishes leading from supervising.

IMPLICATIONS — WHAT THIS MEANS TO YOU

Many individuals feel that past experiences and failures affect their ability to become accomplished leaders. However, studies have repeatedly shown that past events and failures are not indicative of future success in life. Managers who have become effective leaders have learned to put the past behind them. They learn lessons from their negative experiences and move on. Nothing is accomplished by lingering over things that cannot be changed. Leaders learn to focus on the future and on the opportunities that present themselves. They have a vision of where they want to go, and this drives their actions toward the accomplishment of their goals. In order to accomplish this, managers seeking to lead need to develop six personal qualities or traits that are able to enhance their potential.

This is important for managers desiring to establish themselves as effective leaders: if they wish to move ahead in their professional lives and careers, they must always look to the future and not be hindered by past experiences. While nothing can change the past, leaders know they definitely can shape the future.

STRATEGIES, TIPS & TECHNIQUES TO APPLY

In determining individual leadership potential there are six areas that need to be carefully examined.

Perseverance

Managers as leaders must learn to think beyond the horizon. Their vision needs to focus on long-term vantage points in which smaller short-terms goals are used as stepping stones to its attainment. Even though a vision may take several years to attain, effective leadership demands a continual focus on where exactly the manager wants to go. Their vision becomes the driving force that keeps them from becoming sidetracked or distracted by daily problems and issues.

Followed with unwavering perseverance, such foresight equips managers with the discipline and dedication to continually move forward, no matter the obstacles. Knowing at times they may have to take two steps back before being able to take one forward, they are able to stay positive.

Attention to Detail

Managers as leaders must pay attention to smaller details and not just larger more obvious considerations. The process should not become an obsession, but is a necessary requirement if they are to move forward. Success truly is in the details, as carelessness and the need to backtrack to correct faulty procedures, errors or inaccuracies can be extremely costly (in terms of both time and money) from a departmental and organizational standpoint.

Flexibility

In regard to being able to accomplish and attain their goals and personal vision, managers as leaders must be able to drive through obstacles and barriers. Rather than be dissuaded from their goals, they must have the flexibility and resourcefulness to find ways to overcome hurdles and complications.

Managers as effective leaders view overcoming obstacles as challenging opportunities rather than as impossible crises. A flexible attitude and mindset enables them to adapt and modify their plans, and, rather than abandon them, slow down in order to reach certain individual objectives.

Coping

Managers as leaders must learn to view life and the challenges it presents philosophically. If they can do this, they can cope with whatever happens in their jobs as well as personal lives. They must remember that such things as producing exceptional results, meeting timelines and spur-of-the-moment deadlines or exceeding expected quotas does not just happen. As leaders, managers "make things happen," which requires resilience.

Competence

Managers as leaders must keep in mind that learning and developing professional competence is a lifelong pursuit. Education does not end after graduation; knowledge and expertise are continually developed over time. It is critical to maintain an open mind in order to be able to weigh, analyze and consider situations, circumstances and viewpoints objectively and accurately. As all of life is a learning experience, managers as effective leaders must focus on specific rational goals that are able to make them more professional and competent.

Inner Strength

Managers as leaders recognize that their leadership abilities come from within. They must be driven by a personal vision of what they know can be successfully accomplished. It is essential to become "possibility thinkers," always looking for new opportunities for themselves, their organizations and their employees. The inward strength that comes from believing in their personal vision must become the impetus for helping induce others to work collectively together toward their cause.

POINTS TO PONDER – SOMETHING TO THINK ABOUT

1. Do you feel that your leadership ability or personal potential has been hindered due to past experiences and failures?
2. Have you been hindered by the belief that you were not born to be a leader? How has this thinking changed your level of self-confidence or personal acknowledgement of your true capabilities?

TRAINING ACTIVITY – APPLICATION & ACTION PLAN

Determine your own potential as a leader.

1. Create four columns on a sheet of paper. In the first column list the aforementioned six leadership traits.
2. In the second column, list your positive attributes next to each trait.
3. In the third column, list the attributes you need to work on.
4. In the final column, list the actions you need to take to enhance your leadership abilities and potential.

3

Effective Leadership Principles

Good leadership is the result of acting according to reliable practices as well as intuition. Managers as leaders use sound management and leadership principles to guide and direct their actions and activities. They know where they want to go and what specifically needs to be done in order to get there, and that each particular step needs to be carefully considered as to the consequences associated with specific actions and decisions.

IMPLICATIONS — WHAT THIS MEANS TO YOU

As previously discussed, there is a difference between managers who lead and those who supervise. Leaders use sound management and leadership principles as tools to help them achieve their goals and objectives. More traditional managers often attempt to use their authority to protect their "turfs" with little or no regard for the people they are responsible for.

Managers as leaders are driven by a vision of what they want to accomplish. They always have their "eye on the prize" and know just where they want to go and why. They work through their employees using their own passion as a strong motivational tool, demonstrating the possibilities of what all can achieve together.

STRATEGIES, TIPS & TECHNIQUES TO APPLY

Managers as successful leaders must be enthusiastic and positive in all of their actions and interactions. This is demonstrated by the use of the following key leadership principles:

Planning

Planning has suffered with the inception of many 90s management fads. Many in the now defunct dot-com companies proclaimed that planning was an obsolete management function. The accepted view was that circumstances change too quickly to be effectively planned for. They fully believed that it was better to be reactive rather than proactive. The failure of this theory was evident in the bursting of the dot-com bubble.

Good leaders know their success is founded on solid management principles—including planning. They also understand that things are always in flux and changing, and they plan accordingly to anticipate what must be done to accommodate particular changes. They take the necessary time to frequently modify their plans to bring them into line with actual conditions.

Organization

Managers as leaders must understand how to apply and use organizational matrixes to gauge and measure their personal time, efforts and resources as well as those of their employees. Matrixes allow for simultaneous monitoring of various organizational activities across multiple levels.

Effective organizational management provides leaders strategic control over their areas of workplace responsibility. One of their major roles is to manage employees and make certain they are producing ongoing results. Managers are also responsible for the various behaviors and outcomes of the people they manage. This can only be accomplished through effective organizational practices and methods.

Stimulation

Managers who lead must be exceptional motivators. They must learn how to effectively use their passions and visions to attract and motivate others. But as motivation is not enough, they must also use ideas, conceptions and actions to stimulate their employees' thinking and stretch their capabilities. They must make it a point to understand the individuality of everyone they manage and apply different techniques to stimulate and motivate each in the most effective manner.

Information

Leaders are always mindful of the power that information has on their personal ability to perform effectively. Today, too many managers are awash in information, while starving for expertise.

Leaders must be able to distill the vast flow of information into usable metrics and data, which makes it easier to understand what is happening within their organizations. Detailed informational input should actively support all key management metrics and help keep ongoing tabs on every aspect of employees' important activities. Accessing particular information only when it is required without excessive daily review allows them the freedom to manage effectively without being bogged down by information overload.

Leaders must also understand the need for the free-flow of information between superiors, associates and employees. This allows for effective management and communication on all levels.

Time Management

Time is a limited resource, and managers must be able to use it wisely. They need to employ time-saving techniques such as delegation and empowerment to free themselves from tasks and assignments others can just as easily see to. They should look at every activity to determine whether or not it moves them closer to their goals and vision. Activities that do not fit this criterion should either be delegated or dispensed with.

Idea Development

To be competitive and gain an organizational advantage, managers as leaders must create and develop new ideas and concepts. They should always be looking for new and better approaches and for ways to accomplish more with less. A good way to identify and implement ideas, methods or concepts is to brainstorm with associates or employees to determine ways to gain even the smallest marketplace advantage.

Value

Managers as leaders must understand that maintaining and nurturing customer relationships has considerable organizational value. As nothing can be taken for granted, repeatedly meeting and exceeding customers' expectations becomes a top priority. When customer satisfaction is achieved, value is delivered. Managers must incorporate the fact that there will be no compromise on value into their vision statement. Satisfied customers make their professional existence possible.

Efficiency

Effective managers know it takes little extra time and effort to do things right the first time, while carelessness wastes a great deal of time and valuable resources. All organizations have limited resources and managers must work hard to maximize return on investments with those assigned to them. They must make it a point to always look for ways to increase their organizational efficiency, productivity and profitability.

POINTS TO PONDER — SOMETHING TO THINK ABOUT

1. As a manager, what strategies do you employ in order to lead more effectively?
2. How do you use your vision and passion to motivate employees?

TRAINING ACTIVITY – APPLICATION & ACTION PLAN

Determine specific leadership principles to improve upon. On a sheet of paper conduct an analysis.

1. Create three columns and head them "Leadership Principles," "Current Situations" and "Future Activities."
2. In the first column, list the eight principles detailed within this lesson.
3. In the second column, describe a current situation specifically relating to each principle.
4. Detail what you are doing and how you are applying each principle.
5. In the third column, describe activities you can undertake to polish and improve your weaker leadership skill areas.

4

Elements of a Successful Leadership Style

Managers as leaders must learn to work through employees to produce optimal organizational results. In order to do this, they need to develop styles that successfully bring their employees into a "unity of purpose" and motivate them to persevere through challenges, transitions and changes. As part of their leadership styles, they must incorporate practices to reduce and eliminate hindrances and barriers to their effectiveness. As leaders, they willingly help employees succeed in all of their efforts and activities.

IMPLICATIONS — WHAT THIS MEANS TO YOU

There are many managers who choose to focus only on the negative aspects of their employees' performance. When accomplishments are attained in a timely and efficient manner, they minimize them rather than use recognition and praise to build motivation and future success. They feel that when negative aspects are strongly emphasized, employees will work harder to attain the expected level of performance. While this may work for some employees, it tends to demoralize the majority.

As individual employees are unique, different approaches tend to motivate them successfully. Positive motivation and feedback are two powerful ways to maximize their personal results. As leaders, managers remember that success is built upon success, and that individual employees want to be valued for their positive and ongoing contributions.

STRATEGIES, TIPS & TECHNIQUES TO APPLY

Personal leadership styles vary with the personalities and experiences of individual managers. However, in order to attain maximum results from their employees, there are essential elements that need to be incorporated into all leadership styles.

Avoid Negativity

Many managers believe it is more motivating to continually focus on what employees are doing wrong. By maintaining a focus on the negative aspects of employee abilities, attitudes, performance and skills, they assume individuals will work harder to correct them. This is an outmoded style widely used by managers in the 1950s through the 70s and even into the 80s. It was ineffective then, and is certainly so in today's work climate.

Managers who lead refrain from continually telling employees what they did wrong. This is not to overlook negative areas of performance. That which is observable in terms of an employee not completing assignments in an efficient, timely and correct manner indicates the need for additional training and instruction. Effective managers thoroughly train their employees in how to do things properly. If negative behaviors or outcomes persist with individual departmental or unit members, leaders should consider employing individual coaching techniques in order to bring them up to par.

Learn from Mistakes

Many traditional managers have a zero-tolerance rule for mistakes and failures. They often have the unrealistic expectation that employees should robotically analyze everything to preclude the possibility of making any errors. This creates a stressful work environment that encourages covering up errors in judgment and assignment failures. Because work environments become severely restrictive, employees are also reluctant to report any negative marketplace news, trends and indicators they observe. Consequently, demanding managers often end up isolated and far removed from valuable sources of information and feedback, to the effect that many are surprised and placed into reactionary states when unanticipated events and circumstances surface.

As part of their leadership styles, managers must emphasize the value of learning from mistakes and failures. They need to encourage employees to openly report and share inaccuracies in information, faulty decisions and their consequences, and judgment errors and their repercussions with others so that all can benefit from the lessons learned.

Point Out Mistakes and Move on

As a leadership principle, managers need to view mistakes and failures as opportunities for improvement and growth. Rather than rebuke and upbraid them, they help employees analyze particular missteps or failures and distill the lessons to be learned. This allows employees to move ahead consistently and effectively. They understand that nothing is to be gained from worrying over past mistakes: the only thing that matters is correction and positive future performance.

Avoid Unfair Comparisons

Every employee has a unique set of skills and motivations. There are a number of factors that directly affect individual performance, including organizational opportunities and skill/competency levels. It is unfair to compare one employee's continuous performance with another's. This generally carries demoralizing and de-motivating consequences and effects.

Evaluating individual performance from an unbiased professional standpoint is part and parcel of an effective leadership style. The only fair comparison lies in analyzing the employee's previous and ongoing personal work record and results. Doing this affords valuable insights into areas of weakness and opportunities for professional growth. As individual performance must be reviewed with all controllable and uncontrollable factors considered, managers should factor in any organizational changes or transitions that may have impacted certain areas of performance.

Have an Action Plan

Leaders cannot manage any of their responsibilities effectively without a plan. They need to go beyond the scope of typical annual planning. When they encounter problems, tasks or assignments, they need to focus on creating an action plan to achieve optimum results. This includes addressing:

- Goals
- Communication
- Accountability
- Follow up

Learn to LISTEN

As part of their leadership style, managers must learn to listen carefully to what individual departmental or unit members have to say. They must be able to develop complete knowledge of situations and circumstances before making judgments or offering advice. Clear understanding must then be followed up with positive action.

POINTS TO PONDER – SOMETHING TO THINK ABOUT

1. Have you ever used negative motivational techniques? What were the results?
2. Do you hold to a zero-tolerance policy for mistakes? If so, what results do you see?

TRAINING ACTIVITY – APPLICATION & ACTION PLAN

1. Perform a personal assessment by list the following elements on a sheet of paper:

- Experiencing negativity or reacting negatively
- Covering up mistakes
- Dwelling on mistakes
- Making unfair comparisons
- Not developing continuous action plans
- Not listening carefully

2. Rate yourself on a scale of 1 to 5, with five being the highest, where certain actions or behaviors frequently occur. Identify weaker areas and develop strategies to strengthen them.

5

The Art of Becoming a Leader

Managers who lead seek out opportunities, evaluate their potential and take decisive action to either pursue them or not. In order to involve employees in the process and instill a sense of unified, collective effort, managers depend upon their personally consistent, determined and trustworthy leadership styles.

Leadership styles should not be confused with attitudes. Some managers adhere to restrictive and bureaucratic styles to compel employees to produce results. They are unable to tolerate failure and mistakes. The resulting attitudes they display suggest that they believe no one else in the work environment is as important, indispensable and powerful as they are.

Managers as leaders work with and through their employees. They use their leadership skills to identify opportunities and motivate their department or unit members to achieve increased results through appropriate and decisive action.

IMPLICATIONS – WHAT THIS MEANS TO YOU

All leaders tend to develop their own individual, comfortable ways of getting things done. Some managers believe their styles reflect how they personally act and respond, when in fact they are simply based on how they prefer to function within roles, assignments and responsibilities. Though leadership styles vary, all have specific elements that ultimately define success or the lack thereof.

This is important for managers desiring to become effective leaders. Successful leaders employ a results-oriented style that both motivates individual employees to stretch their abilities and communicates a passion for the accomplishment of their vision. More importantly, effective styles incorporate specific elements to ensure leadership success.

STRATEGIES, TIPS & TECHNIQUES TO APPLY

Managers who desire to become effective organizational leaders need to develop comfortable individualized styles for achieving results and actualizing their visions. This includes:

Being Continually Prepared

Most organizations are experiencing rapid changes due to the thrust of technology and volatile market conditions. Traditional supervising managers often tend to wait for events to occur and conditions to change before taking action. Consequently they are always a step or two removed from being on top of things and taking control of situations. This results in an ongoing series of reactionary moves and positioning strategies.

Leaders, on the other hand, make it a point to anticipate trends and economic conditions and are always prepared to make a move once they sense the timing is right. They are prepared to take the necessary steps to address challenges head on, and have defined specific ways to meet them. They don't wait for conditions to improve or opportunities to open up before they begin to pursue their course.

Continually Acquiring Knowledge

Managers who lead understand the need for continuous learning and the ongoing search for professional knowledge. They know that knowledge combined with expertise turns risks into acceptable opportunities.

While many people tend to judge managers' actions as peril-ridden and hazardous, in reality most are averse to risk taking. They take great care to explore all opportunities and carefully analyze and calculate all involved risk factors. Leaders only move when they know the risks involved are minimized and that the odds of obtaining positive outcomes are in their favor. What appears to be venturesome behavior is actually decisive action, as they only act on their evaluations and analysis after they have reviewed all the facts.

Seeking Out All Available Opportunities

Opportunities can take different forms, not all of which are obvious or readily observable. Careful tracking of industry and economic trends produces indicators of future behavior that may present lucrative openings. Always on the alert for subtle opportunities, they make it a point to anticipate, prepare for, and take advantage of each one when the time is right.

Using Appropriate Timing Factors

Managers are decisive in their actions—not rash. Before specific actions are taken, great care is taken to observe trends and opportunities and weigh them to determine appropriate and effective timing factors. If mistakes are made in timing, judgments are generally not far off. This is an important element in market-sensitive, volatile times.

Making Hard Choices

Managers understand that opportunity is often accompanied by difficult choices. Rapid changes in market or customer conditions may require them to make choices that directly shift focus and resources to more profitable departmental pursuits and away from certain activities or existing methods that produce languishing or diminishing results or profitability.

Developing Persuasive Ambition

Managers who lead have an inexhaustible drive that allows them to take control of situations and events in order to make things happen. Their ambition is limited only by their vision of the things that can be accomplished and how they can go about achieving them. Their foresight is not viewed from a personal standpoint, but is based upon overall cooperative employee effort.

Managers are always looking for ways to motivate and make things happen through persuasive, determined and passionate leadership.

Sharpening Intuitions

Leaders develop a heightened sense of intuition that assists them in identifying trends and opportunities. Their intuition is fine-tuned through personal experiences and by learning from the successes and failures of others.

Being Decisive

Action-oriented by nature, managers who lead are proactive rather than reactive. Neither rash nor indiscriminate, they use objective facts, input, and evaluative processes as well as their intuition to spot trends and possible opportunities. Once they determine that the odds of obtaining positive results from specific opportunities are in their favor, they take immediate action to pursue them.

POINTS TO PONDER — SOMETHING TO THINK ABOUT

1. Would you describe yourself as a proactive or reactive manager? Why?
2. How do you determine whether some opportunities are better than others to pursue?

TRAINING ACTIVITY — APPLICATION & ACTION PLAN

Determine your current status regarding each of the following elements, and whether actions are needed to improve any of them.

- Being Continually Prepared

- Continually Acquiring Knowledge
- Seeking Out All Available Opportunities
- Using Appropriate Timing Factors
- Making Hard Choices
- Developing Persuasive Ambition
- Establishing sharpened intuitions
- Being Decisive

6

How Leaders Develop Trust

One of the pillars of leadership is developing and fostering a deep sense of mutual workplace trust. One of the most vexing problems faced in organizations is a simple lack of trust between employees and their managers. For managers to experience successful growth and positive results in their respective department or unit, trust must be established on all levels. Without a deep sense of trust, their vision, goals and plans—as well as unified workplace cohesion—will be unobtainable.

IMPLICATIONS – WHAT THIS MEANS TO YOU

Establishing trust is difficult, time-intensive work. It is earned when synergistic working relationships are established with individual employees. These relationships are characterized by active communication and listening, open and candid interactions, and a total acceptance of all persons as unique individuals. Trust also includes the manager's personal involvement in ensuring employee as well as departmental success.

The fact that managers are granted authority over employees does not guarantee trust between both parties. Trust is based upon truth, which implies open, honest and direct communication free of personal or hidden agendas. For managers to become totally effective leaders trust must be earned and established. In the absence of trust, leadership principles will be of little consequence in the workplace.

Managers have a unique role within organizational workplaces. While they are responsible for individual employees and are required to guide and direct their activities, many are working on different assignments, projects and tasks in varying phases of completion. Many times it becomes impossible for managers to oversee everyone's ongoing daily activities. This type of environment demands that high levels of trust are established and sustained.

Lack of trust in the workplace stems from areas managers can fall short in, including:

Establishing a Work Environment Free of Fear

Most managers are generally under extreme pressure to produce ongoing results. Many are focused on agendas that are able to secure or enhance their chances of organizational advancement. In the process, they often create zero-tolerance policies for mistakes and failures. This produces work atmospheres where employees become afraid to discuss problems or results in honest and open dialogue. Rather than trust their managers to support them, they hide pieces of information or mistakes that can hurt or jeopardize them in any way.

Communicating with Employees

Many managers have direct contact with their employees, but often fail to actively listen and engage in conversations that encourage interaction, feedback or input. Some are only interested in picking out certain information that they want to hear without thoroughly listening to anything else being said. Even though they fully believe they are communicating effectively, selective listening and targeted talk work to demoralize their employees and reduce their levels of trust and loyalty.

Interacting in Person

Many managers choose to communicate with their employees via email, written memos or posted messages. Very few efforts are made to interact directly with them on a regular and active basis. This becomes a major pitfall, as only when they make it a point to seek out employees to have open and free discussions and conversations can they become attuned to workplace problems, concerns, and attitudes and know which motivational methods need to be applied to whom.

All employees must be treated fairly, compassionately and honestly and be appreciated for their own particular characteristics and personalities. All have unique needs that must be addressed and met if they are to feel an important part of the organizational team. Since many tend to function with daily frustrations and pressures associated with their assignments and responsibilities, managers as leaders must become actively involved with them daily in order to encourage and sustain the motivation needed to assure they do not succumb to burnout and other psychological problems.

Specific Steps to Building Trust

If leaders wish to establish and build workplace trust, there are specific behaviors that must be avoided.

Criticism – Discussions concerning documented performance results and how to improve them are always necessary and appropriate as one of the manager's primary responsibilities and functions. However, they must make it a point to avoid making unwarranted negative comments regarding an employee's performance, attitudes and decisions, as they are directly perceived as personal criticisms, not constructive performance or work-related input.

Psychological Analysis – Managers as leaders must avoid assuming the role of amateur psychiatrist and analyzing employees' motivations and behaviors. This includes resisting the urge to prejudge their circumstances, situations and actions.

Advice – Managers can easily provide solutions or advice without making the effort to seek employee input. As problems are often more complex than they appear, managers can short-circuit the learning process and alienate employees by not allowing them to identify why things happened, how ineffective solutions were reached, or the particular factors that contributed to inferior results. It is important that managers seek employee input in regard to specific problems in order to understand, analyze and learn from the facts and pertinent information they possess. Only then do they provide their advice, suggestions or solutions.

Command – Some managers tend to coerce, manipulate and force employees into completing assignments on time or accepting increased responsibility. As leaders, they need to avoid these types of actions, and instead motivate and encourage their employees to achieve desired results and/or increase their personal effectiveness and efficiency. They must know their employees well enough to be able to match the appropriate motivational strategy with each individual.

Control – Managers as leaders must avoid controlling actions and behavior through intimidation techniques and practices. Threatening employees with negative consequences does not motivate them. Employees need to be consistently and positively encouraged to produce results. Intimidation only serves to demoralize them.

Intense Questioning – Managers as leaders must avoid second-guessing and questioning employees on every decision, idea, recommendation or suggestion they make. Employees must be trusted to make decisions on their own without intense scrutiny and oversight. A barrage of suggestions or intense questioning as to their employees' rationale or methods on every assignment only creates more obstacles to them doing their jobs properly, and sends a clear message that their manager thinks them untrustworthy and even incompetent.

POINTS TO PONDER – SOMETHING TO THINK ABOUT

1. Do you tend to have a trusting or mistrusting attitude toward employees?
2. Is your management style built on allowing employees enough freedom to do things their way, or is it more on controlling and directing their activities and procedures?

TRAINING ACTIVITY — APPLICATION & ACTION PLAN

1. Determine whether employee trust is being hindered or jeopardized. Analyze the following factors:
    - Your work climate and environment
    - Your communication
    - Your personal interaction
    - Your treatment of individual employees
    - Your level of personal involvement
2. Identify areas that may be undermining elements of employee trust. Create strategies to change the overall work climate from "trust-busting" to "trust-building."

7

Improving Your Departmental and Unit Performance

Managers as leaders must move employees forward to improve their overall performance. Due to the diverse nature of most tasks, assignments and projects, this can only be effectively accomplished by working individually with each employee. It is important to remember that all individual employees have a part and role to play in the successful achievement of overall departmental goals and objectives.

IMPLICATIONS – WHAT THIS MEANS TO YOU

Managers as leaders realize that one of their main functions is to develop and grow their employees into their own leadership roles in the organization. It is not enough to simply guide and direct department or unit activities; managers must actively work with their individual employees to assess their skills and assist in providing ways to improve upon them. Additionally, effective leaders nurture their employees along the way to achieving long-term professional goals and associated organizational targets.

This is important for managers to appreciate: when they help their individual employees grow and achieve long-term developmental goals, they will be more motivated to produce ongoing job-related results. They will see that there is a plan to follow in order to achieve their desired objectives and results. Every task and activity takes on a personal significance as an additional step to achieving desired personal goals.

STRATEGIES, TIPS & TECHNIQUES TO APPLY

Managers and employees must develop performance partnerships that result in individual long-term growth and development. This is accomplished through use of a performance improvement model that encompasses measuring, analyzing and evaluating personal abilities and growth potential within individual departments and units. Once individual performance plans are developed, employees are empowered to control their own growth and development. Managers as leaders assume the role of coaches and motivators, assisting each employee in achieving their individualized goals and objectives. This coaching includes:

Skill Appraisal and Development

The initial step in developing a performance improvement model is to evaluate the specific skill levels of each employee. Managers need to both identify and correlate these levels with long-range professional organizational goals. Together, individual employees and managers map out long-term developmental plans. One of the purposes of this evaluation is to benchmark individual performance in order to measure increases or decreases throughout the performance improvement model.

The plan should provide individual employees with specific goals, objectives and milestones needed to achieve their long-term professional objectives and goals. Specific rewards, advancements, pay increases or potential promotions are then directly linked to the meeting of specific targets.

Skills Training

The second aspect of the performance improvement model is to determine specific skills training and coaching that each employee may require. In many instances, training can be provided for multiple employees with similar needs. In other instances, specific training or coaching may be required for the remediation or the enhancement of specific but necessary skills.

In some instances a learning acquisition plan providing structured training and coaching over a specified period of time may be called for. In this manner, employees are provided with the individual tools they need to accomplish their professional goals and improve their overall job-related performance.

Performance Application

Once skills training and coaching have been consistently delivered to individual employees, it becomes their responsibility to apply and implement the skills acquired. Employees can only assume ownership of newly acquired skills by immediately applying them to their daily work activities and responsibilities. Without regular use and reinforcement, the skills will be quickly forgotten.

Employees must be evaluated on their specific actions and results, as these are initial indicators of their personal attitudes, motivation and willingness to achieve their determined goals, objectives and plans. At this point managers can only motivate their employees. Employees alone must assume full responsibility and accountability for their personal actions and performance.

Feedback and Reinforcement

Shortly after employees receive training, managers must offer performance feedback and reinforcement to assure that the acquired skills are applied and reinforced. Numerous surveys indicate that any training that is not reinforced is forgotten within 30 days. Managers that wish to move their department members toward the accomplishment of specific performance goals and objectives need to ensure that all skills training is adequately reinforced and properly as well as consistently applied.

Performance Measurement

Within four to six weeks after training has been received, managers need to perform an initial assessment of each employee's progress toward their goals and milestones. As new skills are applied and reinforced, there should be a noticeable improvement in their overall performance.

Performance Appraisal

Managers should conduct performance appraisals quarterly to again measure individual progress. At this stage managers should be seeking ways to actively assist employees in achieving their goals and assessing whether additional skills training, coaching or other assistance is needed to make them more successful in their efforts. The purpose is to ensure progress is being achieved and to remove any obstacles or barriers from their personal development and work-related paths.

POINTS TO PONDER — SOMETHING TO THINK ABOUT

1. How do you move your employees ahead toward accomplishing development goals and objectives?
2. Have you previously used developmental goals as motivational tools for employee growth and performance improvement?

TRAINING ACTIVITY — APPLICATION & ACTION PLAN

Develop a performance improvement plan for your employees.

1. Evaluate and benchmark each individual employee's skill and performance levels.
2. Determine the specific training, coaching and mentoring each requires.
3. Meet with each employee and agree upon a performance improvement plan that satisfies his or her long-term professional goals.
4. Create a training schedule around individualized goals and milestones and that includes performance reinforcement activities, measurements and appraisals.

8

Polishing Leadership Skills

Leadership is not a term to use loosely. Managers as leaders are constantly seeking ways to enhance their abilities, learn new skills, and apply and polish them. Leadership is an ongoing process, attitude and state of mind. Effective leaders always look for opportunities to broaden their horizons and serve their associates, subordinates and customers.

IMPLICATIONS — WHAT THIS MEANS TO YOU

Many managers wish they could become effective leaders. While there are natural leaders, many have learned then applied and honed effective leadership skills. It is a conscious decision to motivate and discipline oneself to make the transition.

Anyone with the desire can make the changes needed to become an effective leader. While some leaders are charismatic, most are not. Often the result of a definite change in personal attitude, they simply took the time to learn, apply and polish their skills.

STRATEGIES, TIPS & TECHNIQUES TO APPLY

The traditional management approach is tactical, directing and controlling their department's daily activities. The leader's perspective is always long-term, seeking ways to increase performance and add value to their company.

Managers who want to polish and hone their leadership skills undertake the following steps:

Understand the Entire Business

Leaders recognize the need to understand their entire business. This includes an intimate knowledge of their company, customers and industry. Only when they fully understand their business can they think strategically. This allows them to gain an overall perspective and objective insights into what is happening in all aspects of their business. Their vision of what the company is capable of, and their role in it, stems from this knowledge and expertise.

Managers as leaders look at everything as a learning experience. They read every industry book, trade journal and magazine. They actively engage in conversations and discussions with knowledgeable people and maintain an open mind. They continually look for new insights and expertise to broaden their knowledge base and skill level.

This comprehensive, wide-ranging view of their business has additional benefits. Individuals with intense insight become extremely valuable to their employer. Having the ability to view things objectively from various perspectives, while analyzing situations thoroughly and in-depth, makes them highly desirable members of any management team.

Network

Leaders actively network with their customers, prospects, associates, superiors and subordinates. They actively work to develop networks of people for personal support, business development and an open exchange of ideas.

Take on Extra Responsibilities

Leaders are always seeking additional responsibilities and experiences to broaden their horizons and enhance their professional capabilities. These are "possibility thinkers" who have a positive and productive attitude. New and additional responsibilities are their way of personally impacting the results and profitability of the company.

Consequently, managers who lead are the first people thought of when new projects, tasks and promotions become available.

Have the Desire

Leaders have a burning desire to succeed and are passionate about and driven by their personal vision. They actively and continually "talk up" their vision, ideas and company with associates, subordinates and customers. This passion builds their self-esteem and assurance, producing a quiet confidence and strong sense of purpose.

Develop Self-Awareness

Leaders are fully aware of their personal strengths and weaknesses. This self-awareness produces a continual drive for improvement. Managers as leaders are constantly appraising themselves, building on their strengths and taking action to address their weaknesses or shortcomings.

When leaders adhere to these principles, they naturally increase their professional value and desirability as an employee. Though this is the positive result of the development of effective leadership skills, it is not the personal motivation behind most leaders. Leaders are motivated by the challenge of building an organization and molding their own employees into leaders. They rise above the politics of their organization and focus on the results they can produce and the impact they can have.

POINTS TO PONDER – SOMETHING TO THINK ABOUT

1. Do you have a personal desire to become a more effective leader?
2. What have you personally done to build, apply and polish your leadership skills?

TRAINING ACTIVITY — APPLICATION & ACTION PLAN

Develop a leadership plan for yourself.

1. Determine what you need to do to learn everything you can about your company.
    a. Who do you need to talk to?
    b. What publications do you need to read?
    c. What industry trends do you need to know more about?
    d. What methods and processes do you need to find out more about?
2. Determine if there are extra responsibilities you can undertake.
    a. What are they?
    b. What extra effort would they require?
    c. How would go about them?
3. Determine how to increase your personal desire.
    a. What motivates you?
    b. What are your personal goals?
    c. What do you need to do to spur yourself on?
4. Develop self-awareness.
    a. What are your personal and professional strengths?
    b. What are your weaknesses?
    c. What do you need to do to improve?
5. Increase your networking.
    a. What is your main purpose for wanting to network?
    b. What can you do to increase your networking activities?
    c. Who do you want to meet?
    d. How will you meet them?

About the Author

Timothy F. Bednarz, Ph.D. is CEO of the American Management Development Group, Inc. For over 20 years he has researched, designed and authored hundreds of learning and development programs used by Fortune 1000 companies.

He is also the author of *Great! What Makes Leaders Great. What They Did, How They Did It and What You Can Learn from It* (2011).

Speaking Availability

Timothy F. Bednarz, Ph.D. is available for speaking engagements for your next meeting or association event. He can be contacted at 800-654-4935 or by e-mail at timothy.bednarz@majorium.com.

Bulk Sales

Bulk sales of this book or any other titles available from Majorium Business Press. Inquiries can be directed to sales@majorium.com, or by phone at 800-6654-4935.

Quick Order Form

Fax orders: 715-342-1118. Send this form.

Telephone orders: Call 800-654-4935 toll-free. Have your credit card ready.

Email orders: sales@majorium.com

Postal orders: Majorium Business Press, 2025 Main Street, Stevens Point, WI 54481, USA.

Please send the following books:

____

____

____

____

Please send more FREE information on:

❑Catalog ❑Speaking/Seminars ❑Mailing Lists ❑Consulting

Name: ____

Address: ____

City: __________________________ State: _____ Zip: __________

Telephone: ____

Email address: ____

Sales tax: Please add 5.5% for products shipped to Wisconsin addresses.

Shipping by air:

United States: $4.00 for first book and $2.00 for each additional product.

International: $9.00 for first book; $5.00 for each additional product (estimate).

Made in United States
Cleveland, OH
05 November 2026

47675528R00030